Marco Marker
He's a joker who loves messing about, but he always means well, even if he sometimes gets things wrong.
Philippa Feltpen
A real peacemaker, she helps keep the other Pens in order by sorting out arguments and giving good advice.
I love Christmas, don't you, Splodge?
Waxy Max
He's very sporty and football mad. On the outside, he's tough, but underneath he's got the biggest heart.
Enter ...
Squiggle and Splodge
The Scribble twins! They're both quiet, both shy. Although they may not look alike, they do almost everything together.

Helping you to get to know God more

Christmas

Written by
Alexa Tewkesbury

It's Christmastime in Pens' town and something special is about to happen. Sharpy's friends are busy getting ready, but he's not sure what for! A short story followed by five days of Bible readings, thoughts and prayers, based on the birth of Jesus, to help young children discover the meaning of Christmas.

What's inside?
Page 4
The Christmas Whisper
Page 22
One Starry Night – Happy birthday, King Jesus!

There was a whisper across Pens' town.

A whisper of excitement.

Sharpy sat at the top of the stairs, pricked up his ears and listened.

'I've got to have the right costume,' he heard Max hiss to Denzil.

'I've got to make some wings,' he heard Marco chuckle to Charlotte.

'I've got to learn my words,' he heard Gloria fuss to Squiggle and Splodge.

Then – 'If everyone's ready,' he heard Philippa announce, 'we can start our rehearsal.'

'Rehearsal?' Sharpy wondered. 'Rehearsal for what?'

There was a whisper across Pens' town.

A whisper of delight.

Sharpy curled up beside the sofa and tried to have a snooze. But he couldn't. Not even for a moment. There was far too much going on.

Some Pens were busy sewing. Some were busy painting.

Some were *so* busy, they forgot to have lunch!

'How can you be too busy for lunch?' Sharpy frowned to himself. 'Pens are *never* too busy for lunch. And WHAT,' he wanted to know, 'are they all so busy doing?'

There was a whisper across Pens' town.
A whisper of fun.
Sharpy lay down under the table and watched as Charlotte and Denzil spread some odd-looking clothes out on the sofa. There were bright colours and dark colours, plain cloth, checks and stripes.

'Come and try on your costumes,' invited Charlotte. 'They're all finished.'

With some tugging, twisting and tying, Pens managed to wriggle and giggle their way into the odd-looking clothes.

'We look splendid!' beamed Gloria.

'Yes, you do,' agreed Sharpy to himself. 'But splendid for what?'

There was a whisper across Pens' town.
A whisper of wonder.
Sharpy snuggled up by the fire for a quiet five minutes when –
What do you think?

Marco twirled round the room a few times to give everyone a good look. On his back, he was wearing WINGS! He'd cut them out of big pieces of card and painted them all white and feathery.

'Perfect!' cried Pens.

'You look wonderful, Marco!' smiled Gloria. 'Just like an angel.'

'But why is he wearing wings?' Sharpy grunted to himself. 'And WHAT'S AN ANGEL?'

There was a whisper across Pens' town.
A whisper of joy.
Sharpy sat down by the front door, watching.
'Have we got everything?' asked Philippa.

'I've got the star,' replied Max. He'd made a star shape out of twigs and painted it gold.

'I've got the manger,' answered Denzil. He pointed to a box he'd filled with straw.

'We've got the baby,' said Squiggle and Splodge. Splodge cuddled a small blanket, all bundled up as if there were a baby tucked inside.

'Then I think we're ready,' Philippa declared.

Sharpy sighed thoughtfully. 'But ready for WHAT?' he wondered.

There was a whisper across Pens' town.
A whisper of peace.
Sharpy stood by the garden gate. The night sky twinkled with starlight and the air felt frosty and cold.
With everything Pens had made gathered together, Denzil said, 'Let's go!'
'Ready, Sharpy?' called Max. 'You're coming, too.'
They scurried off, with Sharpy padding curiously along behind.
When they reached the school, they slipped inside. The hall was warm and brightly lit – and full of other Pens from Pens' town.
This is it! Time to celebrate a very special birthday.

Birthday?
WHOSE BIRTHDAY?

There was a whisper across Pens' town.
A whisper of hope.

Sharpy waited and listened.

'Are my wings straight?' asked Marco.

'Is my dress on the right way round?' worried Gloria.

'Just one last thing to do,' said Max.

Out of a bag, he pulled a rug. It was soft and white and fluffy. Very gently, he laid it over Sharpy's back and pulled it up to his ears.

'Brilliant, Sharpy!' smiled Max. 'Now you're ready, too.'

Sharpy stood very still, blinking. 'What's brilliant?' he wished he knew. 'And WHATEVER AM I WEARING?!'

'Hello!' Charlotte greeted the audience of Pens in the school hall.
Welcome to the birthday of Jesus – God's Son.

Then Pens' play began!

They told how the baby Jesus was born in a stable because His mother, Mary, and her husband, Joseph, had nowhere else to go; how there was no comfy cot for Jesus to sleep in, just a manger that the animals ate their food from; how God sent an angel to some shepherds inviting them to visit the newborn Jesus; and how a star led some wise men to the little baby lying in the straw.

'Jesus came into the world,' announced Marco the angel, 'so that we can all be God's friends for ever and ever!'

Suddenly –

'Sharpy the sheep!' called Charlotte the shepherd. 'Come into the stable with us.'

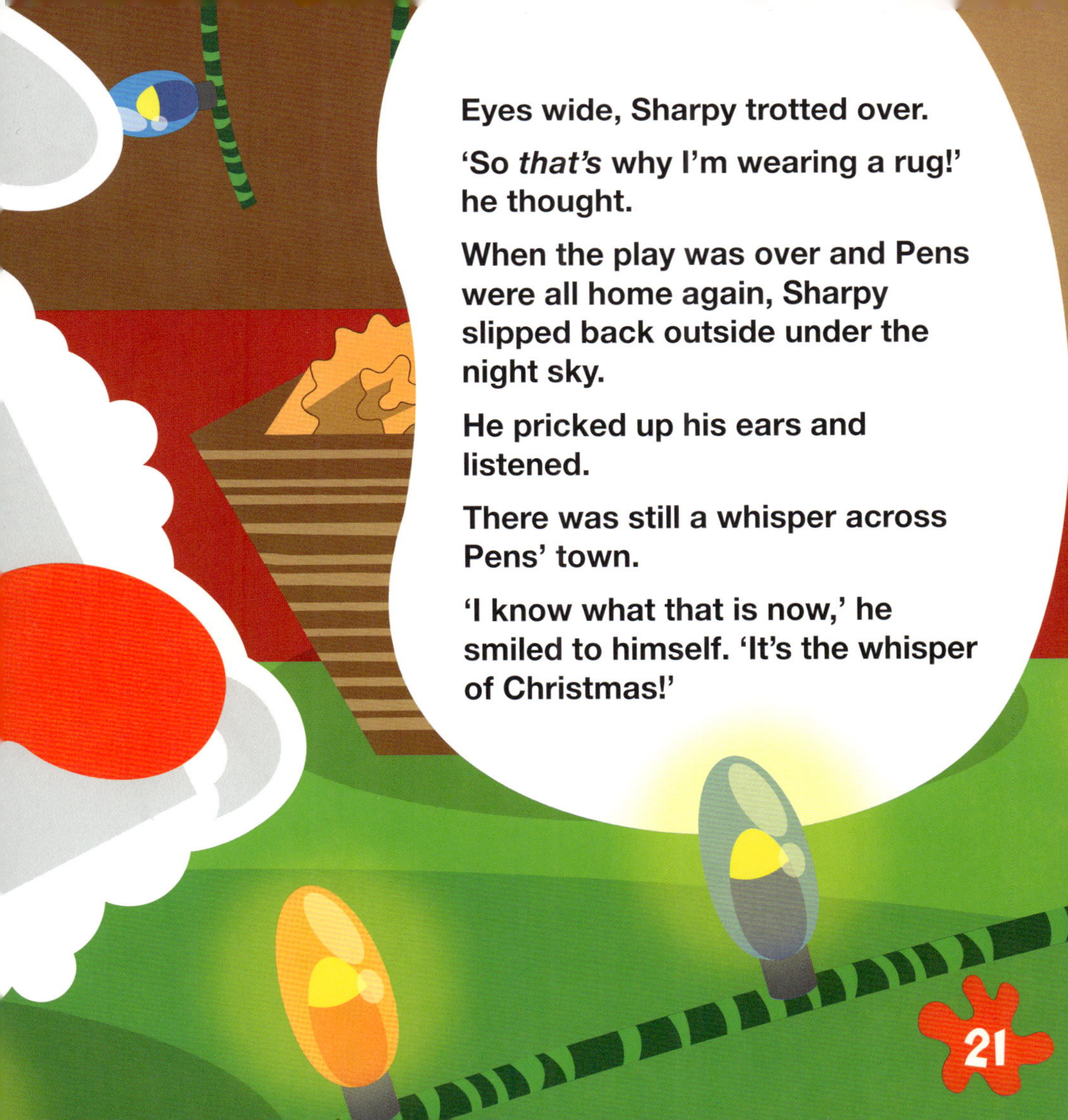

Eyes wide, Sharpy trotted over.

'So *that's* why I'm wearing a rug!' he thought.

When the play was over and Pens were all home again, Sharpy slipped back outside under the night sky.

He pricked up his ears and listened.

There was still a whisper across Pens' town.

'I know what that is now,' he smiled to himself. 'It's the whisper of Christmas!'

ONE STARRY NIGHT
Happy birthday, King Jesus!
Day 1
The wonderful news
'The angel came to [Mary] and said, "Peace be with you! The Lord is with you and has greatly blessed you!"'
(Luke 1 v 28)

'Hello!' cried Gabriel, an excited angel.

'You made me jump!' replied Mary, a surprised young girl.

'You're very special, Mary,' continued the angel, 'and God wants me to give you some WONDERFUL news! He has an amazing present for the world – a new baby, His very own Son. The baby will be King over all the Earth. He will teach everyone about God's love and how to be His best friends for ever! And guess what, Mary?' Gabriel smiled. 'God's chosen YOU to be the baby's mother! You're to give Him the name, Jesus.'

Do you know any babies and when their birthdays are?

Jesus came into the world to bring people close to God.

Pens Prayer

Father God, thank You so much for Jesus, Your amazing present! Amen.

Day 2
Busy in Bethlehem
'... an angel of the Lord appeared to him in a dream and said, "Joseph ... do not be afraid to take Mary to be your wife."' (Matthew 1 v 20)
NO ROOM

God had another message. It was for a man called Joseph.

'God wants you to marry Mary,' an angel said to him. 'Then together you can take care of God's Son.'

When it was nearly time for Mary to give birth to the baby Jesus, Joseph told her, 'The Emperor wants to know how many people there are. We must travel to Bethlehem to be counted.'

But when Mary and Joseph arrived, there were so many people in Bethlehem already that there was nowhere for them to stay.

'I'm so tired,' sighed Mary. 'Whatever shall we do?'

Mary and Joseph were chosen by God to look after His baby Son on Earth.

God chose Mary and Joseph to do something AMAZING. How do you think they felt?

Pens Prayer

Heavenly Lord, please help me always to do as You ask me to – just like Mary and Joseph. Amen.

Day 3
The baby in the Stable
'She gave birth to her first son … and laid him in a manger – there was no room for them to stay in the inn.' (Luke 2 v 7)

A kind innkeeper could see that Mary's baby was soon to be born.

'You need somewhere to rest,' he said. 'All my rooms are full, I'm afraid, but you're welcome to stay in my stable.'

'Oh, thank you!' smiled Joseph. 'I was beginning to think we'd have to spend the night out here in the street.'

So there it was in the innkeeper's stable, among the animals and the piles of straw, that Jesus, the Son of God, came into the world. And Mary laid Him gently down to sleep in the animals' feeding box.

Jesus was born a King, but He came to be everyone's Friend.

Pens Prayer

Dear Lord, this Christmas I praise You for Your Son, Jesus – my special Friend! Amen.

Day 4
Good news!
'Don't be afraid! I am here with good news for you, which will bring great joy to all the people.' (Luke 2 v 10)

That same night, in the fields outside Bethlehem, some shepherds were looking after their sheep.

Suddenly, the sky above them was filled with dazzling light, and an angel appeared!

The shepherds trembled with fright.

'Don't be afraid!' said the angel. 'Listen! God's Son has just been born. He will save people from all the wrong things they do and bring happiness to the whole world. And God's chosen *you*,' the angel beamed, 'to be His first visitors!'

So the shepherds hurried off excitedly. When they found Jesus in the stable, they sang praises to God.

God invited some poor shepherds to be the first to visit Jesus to show that EVERYONE is special enough to meet Him.

Pens Prayer

Father God, just like the shepherds, I'm so excited that You've invited ME to meet with Jesus! Amen.

Day 5
The King's Star
'... the same star ... went ahead of them until it stopped over the place where the child was.' (Matthew 2 v 9–10)

A while afterwards, some wise men saw a brand-new star in the sky.

'That means a new King has been born,' they nodded happily. 'Let's see if the star leads us to Him.'

So off they went, following its path.

At the palace of a king called Herod, they asked about the baby Jesus.

'He's in Bethlehem,' they were told – and the star led them to the exact place!

There, the wise men knelt down and gave God's Son presents of gold and frankincense and myrrh.

They knew that King Jesus was someone very special.

On the very first Christmas, Jesus was born to be Lord of the whole world!

When you wake up on Christmas morning, what could you say to Jesus?

Pens Prayer

I praise you, dear Lord God, for Christmas. Through all the fun and excitement, please help me always to remember that it's Jesus' birthday. Amen.

Other Pens titles

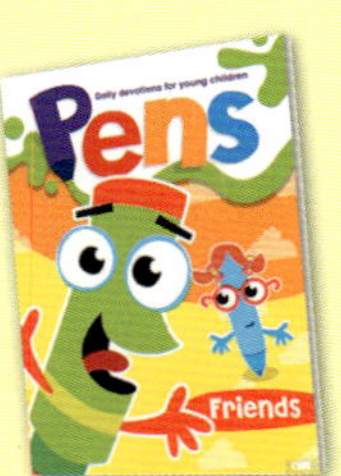

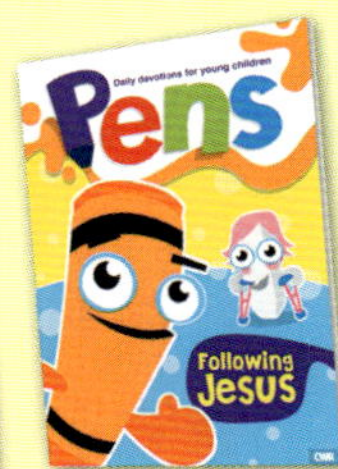

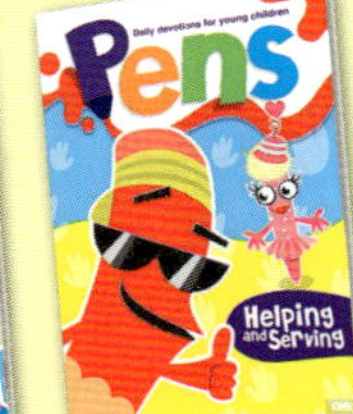

Each book contains 30 days of daily readings, stories, questions and prayers.

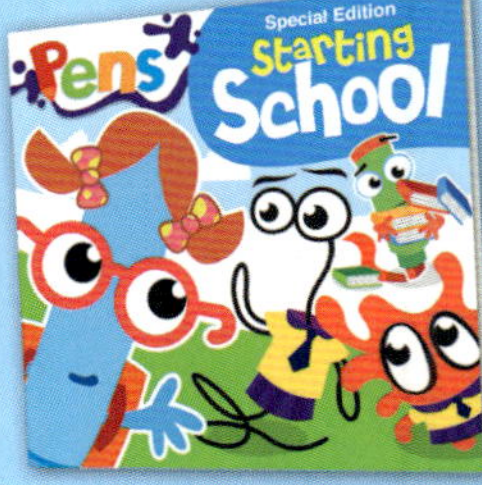

Pens Special! Starting School

Help children start school confidently, knowing that God goes there with them. A short story followed by five days of Bible notes.

For current prices visit
www.cwr.org.uk/store

Available online, from your local Christian bookshop.